SEAFORD MEMORIES
1950 - 1999

Patricia Berry

S.B. Publications

First published in 2003 by S. B. Publications,
19 Grove Road, Seaford, East Sussex BN25 1TP

ISBN 1-85770-286-7

Designed and Typeset by EH Graphics (01273) 515527

CONTENTS

ACKNOWLEDGEMENTS

I acknowledge with gratitude the contributions made by Mr. Gordon Marsh, Mr. R.H.C. Minchin, Mr. Peter Fellows, Miss M. Streeter, Mr Peter White and Mrs Violet Banks, all at Fotobox (Seaford), the many local people whose comments and anecdotes have enlivened the preparation of this book, my family, friends and neighbours for their support and understanding and, last but not least, Lindsay Woods of S.B. Publications for her patience and advice.

Other help, permission to reprint, etc. is acknowledged in the text. Apologies are tendered if any source has not been cleared. I hope readers will not mind seeing their younger selves in these pages, and that no-one will be distressed by finding past friends and family included. I will be happy to supply a copy of any picture of interest to them.

Unless otherwise stated, photographs and postcard views are from my own collection, though many can be found recorded at Seaford Museum in the Martello Tower.

Patricia Berry

27th August, 2003.

INTRODUCTION
PEACE AND
AUSTERITY

At 3 pm on Tuesday 8th May 1945, Prime Minister Winston Churchill - a regular visitor to Seaford both in his "wilderness years" and, on occasion, during the Second World War - made the official announcement that hostilities in Europe were at an end. As he concluded "Advance, Britannia!" the weary people of this country celebrated, unaware that they were to find the early days of peace harder to bear than some of the preceding five and a half years. Meanwhile, the cruel war in the Far East was waged for a further three months, till Japan surrendered on 14th August.

Demobilisation of the millions of men and women in the armed forces began soon after VE (Victory in Europe) Day, but it was to continue for many months. What did our home-coming warriors find on their return, not to mention the evacuated mothers and children who had spent years in areas deemed safer than Frontline Seaford?

88 local service personnel had died and twenty civilians were killed in air-raids. The town's warning siren had sounded 1053 times, with both oil and high-explosive bombs and an incredible estimated total of ten thousand incendiary bombs falling. Perhaps the most chilling were the four low-level machine-gun attacks, in one of which Seaford's chief air raid warden was killed.

Church Street, junction of West Street, bombed sites.

There were a number of bomb-sites and gaps where houses and shops used to be, and the streets still bore evidence of black-out times, with bands of white painted on kerbs, tree-trunks and lamp-posts, while posters continued to remind the population to "Dig for Victory" and that "Careless Talk costs Lives". Public air-raid shelters and emergency water tanks still stood at salient points.

The post-war housing situation was dire: 28 buildings had been totally destroyed by enemy action and a further 54 were deemed beyond repair and had to be demolished, the demand for accommodation was acute. Servicemen whose

Broad Street, looking south from Clinton Place, with white-painted tree trunks, etc.

wives and children had lived with older generations during the war now wanted their own places; bigger houses were divided and sub-divided, so that many young families existed in one or two rooms, with shared kitchen, bathroom and lavatory. The government's short-term solution was the building of estates of

Church Street, (far left) Emergency Water Supply "EWS" tank on bombed site.

Vale Road, junction of Lexden Road, "pre-fab" housing.

temporary, pre-fabricated single-storey homes - the "pre-fabs". Seaford's allocation was erected off Vale Road, much of the work done by former enemy prisoners of war (awaiting repatriation) who were encamped on Castle Hill, Newhaven.

Party for local children, 7th January 1946. Organised by mothers and British Legion Women's Section members.

Rationing of food, clothing and fuel not only continued into peacetime: in some cases the quantities allowed were even smaller, and some items appeared on the list for the first time. All the more creditable, then, that on 7th January 1946 a young people's tea-party was organised by mothers and British Legion Women's Section members. Likewise, though fierce currency regulations were in operation, in August 1947 a party of young Seaforders was invited to stay with families in Holland. Each member of the group took about £7.00. spending money, little enough to buy gifts for their hosts. A reciprocal visit to Seaford was subsequently arranged.

From the late nineteenth century Seaford had been a renowned setting for preparatory and boarding schools, and by the summer of 1939 some thirty were established in the area, from the Ladies' College which came in 1893 to last arrivals such as St. Michael's (1936). Many of them were evacuated out of the target zone during the Second World War, while others closed down. The deserted buildings and playing fields were requisitioned as temporary accommodation for the thousands of troops who would pass through the area in the next six years. Some were treated with scant respect by their short-term occupants: the cricket pavilion of one was blown up, while the attics of another were found to have been used as a store for cigarettes and other goods stolen from army canteens.

Local halls that had likewise been requisitioned for wartime use were found on release to need repairs but, once these were done, the buildings soon reverted to their original purposes. Women's Institute members, for instance, were able to return to their headquarters in Claremont Road while the newly-formed local dramatic society started life in the refurbished Clinton Hall.

Young people from Seaford with their hosts in Holland, August 1947.

A major cause for concern was the state of the sea-wall: little maintenance had been possible during the war years, the beach having been closed off with tank-traps, barbed-wire entanglements and other anti-invasion devices. A four-day storm in October 1945 and another two months later did extensive damage. In the latter, four large sections of wall collapsed, two of them more than 200 feet long. Expert

Wartime canteen in a local requisitioned hall.

Claremont Road, Seaford Women's Institute hall.

advice was sought most urgently, resulting in proposals for a £10,000 improvement scheme, but this came too late to prevent flooding in the lower part of the town in 1949, and was only the beginning of problems for our city fathers.

This, then, was the state of play as we entered the second half of the twentieth century.

Steyne Road, looking south-east, flooded buildings.

THE FIFTIES
RECOVERY AND
CELEBRATION

The new decade began on an optimistic note with the opening of modern council flats built by the Ringmer Building Company on the corner site bombed in August 1943 where had stood Riddle's bakery and Howell's grocery in High Street, with cottages and a fried fish shop in East Street.

A most pressing problem was how to hold off the eternal menace, the sea. The scheme proposed to the local Sea Defence Commissioners by consultant engineers Sir William Halcrow & Partners included repairs and improvements to the promenade wall and retention of shingle on the beach.

35-ton crane at Splash Point, sea defence repairs.

At Splash Point a sudden drop of fifteen feet in the level of the beach was found, and emergency work put in hand. The 35-ton crane supporting the pile-driver necessary for the job was too heavy to stand at the edge of the cliff above, so a gantry was built, enabling the work to be done from the seaward side. Farther east at Hope Gap (reached via South Hill Barn and Hope Bottom) new steps were made, while on the stretch between The Buckle and Claremont Road sheet piling faced with reinforced concrete panels and wooden shuttering with a bull-nose coping was installed by the Demolition & Construction Company (the "D & C").

For years to come, it seemed, the company's equipment was always in action somewhere along the sea-front, and residents found the regular thump of pile-driving as familiar a background noise as the waves themselves. Throughout the decade floods and repairs continued.

Sea defence repairs between The Buckle and Claremont Road.

Never forgotten in those parts was the night in November 1943 when the crew of the Newhaven lifeboat made gallant attempts in appalling conditions, heavy seas and a full southwest gale - at great cost to themselves, including the loss of their signalman and serious injury to several others - to help the 25 men on board the stricken H.M. trawler Avanturine.

Though the road sign warning of "Seven schools in the next half-mile" of Sutton Avenue was still relevant, the description of Seaford as "a windy place full of prep schools" hardly applied any more. Employable young people returned from the war with skills and knowledge not to be wasted on the domestic, odd job kinds of work which had kept so many schools ticking over in the 1930s. The "almost continuous green belt of playing fields" surrounding the town, as described in 1937, was now being eyed by developers as ideal for housing expansion.

One educational newcomer was the Home Economics College which in 1950 moved into Corsica Hall, there to remain for some years with female students from many parts of the world. On Parents' Days, the town centre was brightened by the glowing colours of the visitors' tribal robes and oriental gowns.

1951 was a census year - the first since 1931 - with a population of nine thousand ... and one ... recorded in Seaford.

The Great Exhibition of 1851 had been largely inspired by Queen Victoria's consort Prince Albert, to encourage industrial and technical development; to mark its centenary, and to give the nation a much-needed cheer-up while still in the grip of shortages and making-do, plans for a Festival of Britain were announced. Seaford schools, clubs and other groups came up with ideas such as an exhibition of paintings, a talent competition, a pageant and a table-tennis tournament.

Another highlight of 1951 was a visit by radio personality Richard Dimbleby with the popular B.B.C. programme *Down Your Way*, interviewing local people who then requested favourite records to be played during later transmission. Among Seaford folk featured were Mr. Darwall Smith, principal of St. Wilfrid's Prep School, and staff at Champion Electric Corporation Works in their factory on the corner of The Causeway and Steyne Road. The company began there in 1945 with twelve staff assembling midget radio sets; by the time of Mr. Dimbleby's broadcast, the workforce had grown to 250. Later the same year, the factory was gutted by fire and never used again. The corner site stood empty for over forty years, till Kingswell Court was erected.

Champion Electric Corporation staff, party at The Barn.

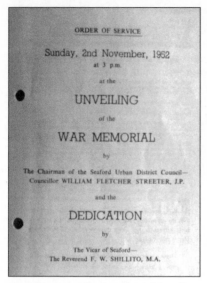

ORDER OF SERVICE

Sunday, 2nd November, 1952
at 3 p.m.

at the

UNVEILING

of the

WAR MEMORIAL

by

The Chairman of the Seaford Urban District Council—
Councillor WILLIAM FLETCHER STREETER, J.P.

and the

DEDICATION

by

The Vicar of Seaford—
The Reverend F. W. SHILLITO, M.A.

Announcement of war memorial unveiling.

On the eastern outskirts of town, the Furniture Trades Benevolent Association had taken over a former girls' school in Sutton Avenue. Back in 1900, as Ravenscroft, it had educated one Margaret Rutherford, later to become the celebrated and much-admired eccentric stage and film character actress. During the First World War, the same premises had been requisitioned as a hospital for wounded Canadian soldiers.

Seven years after the end of the Second World War, the Cornish granite memorial which had stood since 1921 in Dane Road was badly in need of repairs to the damage wrought by the eroding sea-winds. It was also necessary to add to the list of 1914-18 war dead the names of those who died in the later conflict. On 2nd November 1952, following a civic procession, the re-designed memorial was unveiled by Seaford Urban District Council chairman William Fletcher Streeter J.P. at its new site at the junction of Sutton Park Road and Avondale Road. In a poignant ceremony it was dedicated by the Vicar Rev. F.W. Shillito M.A.; church bells rang and wreaths were laid.

Sympathetic enquiries made of the bereaved had ensured such details as the correct spelling of names and the inclusion of "V.C." after the entries for Cuthbert Bromley (Gallipoli, 1915) and Claude Raymond (Burma, 1945). A total of 219 local men and women were recorded, including seven soldiers from the South African (Boer) War and twenty civilian air raid victims, together with the servicemen who died in the two world wars.

A light touch in the dark winter of 1952/3 arose from comments made by the public to the local authority about the "banner with a strange device" being flown from the roof of the Martello Tower by the proprietor of the tea-room within. He explained that it was a Turkish flag, bought secondhand for ten shillings, whereas a new

Grant of Arms, Seaford Council Offices.

Union flag would have cost eight pounds and "been just as much ruined by the winds in one season". The clerk to the council was assured that our own national flag, with many other decorations, would be in place at the Tower in time to celebrate H.M. the Queen's coronation in June 1953.

On 8th April, 1953, a Grant of Arms was made to Seaford Urban District Council, 59 years after its creation. It included the words "E Ventis Vires" ("Strength from the wind"), suggested by Councillor Dinah M. B. Synge. The original document describing the arms in heraldic terms was displayed in the council chamber at Crouch House, where the Council then had its offices. Within 21 years the arms became redundant, when Seaford was made part of the Lewes District.

The Grant of Arms.

Coronation celebrations: the Ritz Cinema decorated.

Celebrating the coronation in 1953, Seaford town centre was bright with bunting and banners, neighbourhood street parties were organised, and a plaque on the wall of the Post Office in Broad Street was unveiled to commemorate the planting of trees. The family firm of B. Berry & Sons of Crouch Lane Smithy made and presented to the town a wrought-iron gate bearing the device "ER II 1953", to be sited within the Tudor stone arch in the East Street wall of the Crouch Gardens, thus symbolically linking the two Elizabethan reigns. With similar sentiment, Seaford Amateur Operatic Society staged Sir Edward German's *Merrie England*, some thirty members taking part.

That same year a shock announcement from the Misses Witherington, Curry and Hodson, principals of

Coronation celebrations: Vale Road street party.

Coronation celebrations: unveiling plaque at Broad Street Post Office.

Seaford Ladies' College, heralded the closure of one of Seaford's first boarding schools. Founded in Beckley, Kent, in 1893 it moved to No. 10 Esplanade, Seaford, but within a short time outgrew those premises and settled finally in Eastbourne Road. Failing health of the principals, escalating running costs and competition from more up-to-date state schools had prompted the decision, taken with pride in the thousands of young women who had been educated there and "left their mark on their generation and influenced girls to follow in their footsteps". A stained glass window depicting left to right) St. Richard, Bishop of Chichester, the Good Shepherd and St. Catherine, with the dedication 'To the glory of God and in memory of Seaford Ladies' College whose members worshipped here 1900 -1953" was installed in the north wall of the Parish Church of St. Leonard.

Coronation celebrations: Berry family's wrought iron gate.

In 1954, after only eight years at the premises in Firle Road, Pilgrims Preparatory School for Boys closed down. It had been acquired by the Rev. G. Randolph after the Second World War, during which the buildings, originally Southlands Girls' School (1924-38) were occupied by a special Army unit, in its latter days manned by members of the A.T.S. The auction of contents of Pilgrims was conducted by the local firm of W. St. John Smith. In 1955, with an official opening by H.R.H. the Princess Margaret, the Invalid Children's Association occupied the buildings as a special school. The Princess made further visits but, under the later name of ICAN (Invalid Children's Aid Nationwide), by 1997 numbers had dropped from 70 to 21 and the unit was no longer viable. Another building in Firle Road to take on a new guise was Arlington House Hotel which in 1954, re-named Blatchington House, was converted into a civil service retirement home.

That year also, Miss Queenie Morling retired after almost half a century - first as a clerk, then as secretary - with the building firm started by her grandfather in 1844. Farewell gifts were presented to her by the oldest employee

Coronation celebrations: Merrie England with Kathleen Marsh as Queen Elizabeth I, John Heritage and Constance Brewer (far right) as Sir Walter Raleigh and Bessie Throckmorton. A Raymond Austen photograph.

Seaford Parish Church, Ladies' College memorial window.

Mr. E. Banks (first from left, front row) before the assembled staff including Captain, the twelve-year-old gelding who had once drawn the carts of building materials. He was the last horse to be shod at Berry's forge in Crouch Lane.

At the Pelham Arms public house, Lower High Street, when Mr. William Minchin was landlord, an art student on holiday in the area offered to paint a mural illustrating an episode in Seaford's murky past. It is evident that the patrons were his models, and the work was completed in six weeks at a few hours a day. Neither mural nor wall exists today.

Local papers in October 1956 reported on the urgent need for a fourth church in the neighbourhood. The population had risen to more than 10,000 people and combined seating at St. Leonard's, St. Peter's, Blatchington and St.

The Crypt and Folly, Church Street.

Members of Seaford Boys' Club with guests from Newhaven.

Andrew's, Bishopstone was only 850. A piece of land at Chyngton had already been acquired; £20,000 would have to be raised for the building.

By the mid-fifties, housing shortages were still a prime concern, though Seaford Council had been able to build homes on the Chyngton Estate; shortages of both labour and materials continued to delay matters. A further 76 homes were envisaged, but there was no indication of when the pre-fabs could be disposed of. The question of keeping chickens in the gardens of council houses needed clarification: the maximum permitted number of birds remained at six, with the keeping of cocks and cockerels prohibited. Young people - the generation born in wartime - came to the fore in the mid-fifties. Members of the Boys' Club held a successful social with female guests from Newhaven, while at the main door of the Senior Modern School in Arundel Road, the first eleven football team posed with their headmaster Mr Price (far right, standing). From 45 High Street, the newsagents shop of Mr and Mrs Winser, their large force of delivery boys gathered for their annual outing, on this occasion to Southsea.

Though B.B.C. television resumed in December 1949, it was the Coronation that prompted a surge in the number of sets acquired, and it was estimated that 20 million people viewed the ceremonies from 2½ million sets; Independent Television began in September 1955. A popular TV programme *What's my Line?* one evening featured Sam Lucas, longshoreman, of Brooklyn Road. "The man who took the name of Seaford into thousands of British homes" failed to outwit the panel with his mime of holding back the flap of a bathing tent; his weather-beaten complexion was too much of a clue to his outdoor life. Television

Seaford Secondary School football First XI.

cameras came to the town in 1959 with Kenneth Horne's quiz *Snakes and Ladders*, staged at the Queen's Hall.

With the expansion of the "Golden Key" and other private housing estates to the east of the old town, there was a desperate need for an additional primary school. Chyngton County Primary was erected on a site in Millberg Road, with Mr. Lilly the first headmaster, and opened on 21st April 1958.

Seaford was treated to a colourful parade in the last year of the decade when the officers and men of "the Two-Ten" local Territorial Army unit were granted the freedom of the town. Among the first to go into France at the beginning of the Second World War, the peacetime "Saturday night soldiers" had earned the admiration and respect of their fellow citizens, who turned out in force for a day of spectacle. After presentation of the silver Freedom Sword, the men marched through the streets with drums beating, flags flying and bayonets fixed, as tradition allowed.

Winser newsagents' delivery boys' outing.

Television shop window, Seaford High Street (by kind permission of Mr. Bussey)

H.R.H. the Princess Margaret opening Pilgrims special school.

Presentation to Miss Queenie Morling on her retirement.

Pelham Arms public house: mural.

St. Luke's Church, Chyngton.

Harvest festival at Chyngton Primary School.

Council houses built.

THE SIXTIES DEMOLITIONS AND INNOVATIONS

Early in the decade Seaford was once more disrupted by floods, though these were at Lewes, where the South Bourne rose, water streaming along the railway tracks at the station to platform level. Not till it subsided could services to and from Seaford be resumed.

Steyne Close & Bramber Close replace Seaside Convalescent Home.

After some ninety years' service to the community in various guises, the Seaside Convalescent Home, facing the sea on land between Crooked Lane and Bramber Road, was demolished. Blocks of flats and cottages were built in its place, creating new areas designated Steyne Close and Bramber Close. First parts of the landmark building had been erected on the ancient site of Hangman's Acre, to accommodate the increasing numbers of convalescents sent to Seaford after illness or surgery. At times so many applications were received that admissions had to be limited to a maximum of four weeks each. Under royal patronage and with leading national dignitaries interested in the home, it was several times extended, the last in 1922. It was nationalised in 1948 and last used as a hospital four years later, after which a few years were spent as a holiday home and similar.

Only four years after the loss of the Home, its original location - an elegant house in the High Street which began life as "Mr. Washer's house", built in 1713 for the master of Sutton Mill - was also pulled down. At other times it had been known as Augusta House and as Talland. When the Home was established there in 1860, it was believed to be the first such "halfway house" between sickness and full health in this country. It was one of the buildings considered by the local branch of the British Legion for its headquarters after the destruction of the Pelham Road premises by enemy bombs in 1942, but Legion members eventually decided on the former Pelham House Private Hotel in Claremont Road, run before the Second World War by Mrs. Clark and Miss Stainbrook, who had

Site of Talland before demolition.

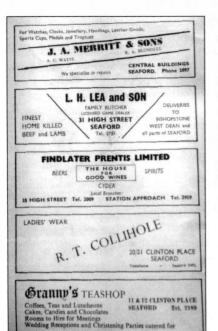
Local traders.

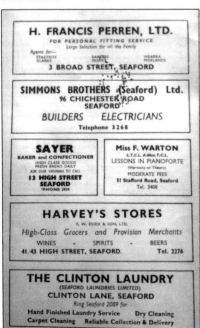

Rotary Club events

Christmas street lighting, 1964.

included "own vegetable produce" in their advertisement in holiday brochures. Earlier still, the Claremont Road building had housed a school for young ladies.

A cinema was another suggestion to replace Talland, but nothing came of that either, and it was not till 1964, after the demolition of Beal's drapery store adjacent to the miller's old house (on the very corner of Lower High Street and Saxon Lane), that shops known as Talland Parade were built on the site.

With some opposition from the town's established provision merchants, Seaford's first self-service grocery store opened at 34 Church Street, formerly occupied by the Misses H. & E. Portsmouth's drapery and outfitters. Though "M and C Stores" may not have been welcomed in some quarters, to the increasing number of housewives holding down full-time office and retail jobs in the town centre (with only the lunch-hour in which to shop and little late-night opening) it was a god-send. Compared with 21st-century superstores, it was small, cramped and primitive, but oh! it was popular.

From time to time, carnivals and similar events were organised; such a one was the Rotary Club's decorated vehicle competition in July 1962, with entrants parading round the town to the delight of onlookers. Rotary also kept up the tradition of Christmas street collections.

At long last, serious plans were being made for the construction of the Buckle bypass, cutting through Hawth Hill and linking Claremont Road and the Newhaven road. This had been an urgent matter on Seaford Urban District Council's agendas for at least fifteen years, during which time a unique emergency scheme operated whenever high seas made the coast road impassable. The landlord of the old Buckle Inn, on judging the moment had come, would activate an illuminated sign placed well in advance of the junction, advising drivers to approach Seaford by an alternative (inland) route.

Work was carried out in 1962-3 and included use of excavated chalk from the hill to infill Valley Dip, prior to building development there. The old Buckle Inn was demolished and a new one erected some yards farther back from the road past the beach. Originally farm cottages, the earlier inn (headquarters for various local groups) had served neighbouring communities Tide Mills,

Seafront road, sometimes threatened by high seas.

Bishopstone and Coast-guards for generations, the Venus family having been landlords for many years. It was said that Mr. Catt, master at Tide Mills, set a rigid curfew on his workers visiting the inn, and would wait under the lantern at the eastern entrance to the village with his watch in hand, ready to challenge those who were late back.

Work on Buckle by-pass.

The old Buckle was close enough to the sea that waves from rough high tides could momentarily submerge the building, washing water and shingle down the chimneys which the occupants then swept out through the front door.

The closure of schools and other major buildings continued through the decade. In 1964 the Downs School for Girls at Sutton Corner ended its stay of more than sixty years, to be occupied as offices of Seaford Urban District Council, moving from Crouch House, Bramber Lane. The coat of arms above the door at the Downs was the work of Mr. Holmes, a teacher at Ladycross School and a Special Constable.

The following year we said farewell to one of our most ancient hostelries, with the destruction of the Old Tree Inn, at the crossroads of High Street with Broad Street/Saxon Lane. Scene of many an election-eve dinner in the pocket borough days when Seaford had its own two Members of Parliament, often chosen after considerable vote-rigging, and of auctions of ship-wrecked goods

Fishermen gather outside the old Buckle Inn.

Old and new Buckle Inns stand together.

and recruiting drives for men who would "take the King's shilling" and go as soldiers in time of war, the building dated back to Tudor times. In those days nearby was the pillory, a T-shaped wooden frame against which a condemned miscreant would be stood, head and hands confined by the upper part of the cross-piece. His fellow townsfolk then showed their disapproval of whatever had been his antisocial behaviour by pelting him with rotten fruit and any other offensive material to hand. At least one such miscreant was in fact female: in 1577 Joan á Wood "a witch" was thus punished.

In modem times there was a convenient short-cut from Upper High Street into Broad Street behind the Old Tree but one took it at the risk of an onslaught to the ears from the mynah bird, kept in a cage in the yard. When a parade of shops was built on the site, the short-cut was replaced by another, but one missed the colourful language.

Front door, Council offices at The Downs.

In March 1966 died Kathleen Ethel, Dowager Duchess of Manchester, of "Ferryden", Green Walk, leaving legacies to a number of local charities. She was the only daughter of Mr. and Mrs. W.H. Dawes of Barn Cottages, Seaford. Mr. Dawes had been general manager at several London theatres including the old Gaiety, and served for two years on Seaford Urban District Council, as well as being Golf Club captain in the 1930s. The Duchess was president of Seaford Flower Club and is buried in the Alfriston Road cemetery.

Three more veteran establishments were to fall to the demolition hammer before the end of the decade. The site of the Crouchfield Hotel at the top of Crooked Lane, its name reminding us of the old tithe map, had been the home of the Danby family; it was acquired as a potential location for a modern replacement for the old Constitutional Club in Church Lane. The Bainbridge Home in Heathfield Road had been established by philanthropist Emerson Bainbridge as a rest centre for shopgirls. Designed in the style of a mountain chalet, the building started life as Switzerland's gallery at the Paris Exhibition of 1900, being taken apart and brought to Seaford thereafter.

In later years the building was used by organisations such as the Grey Ladies' College of Blackheath (whose girls were trained for domestic or agricultural work in the colonies), by girls' groups like the St. John's Church Club of West Ham, and by various benevolent concerns.

Demolition of the Old Tree Inn.

After its destruction houses were built and a new road, Bainbridge Close, came into being.

Out on the western side of town, within the parish of Blatchington, the premises built for the Surrey Convalescent Home more than 75 years before were removed and a residential area created off Surrey Road. Some of the Portland stone incorporated in the original staircase at the home was part of the cargo from the Mary Davies, stranded on the beach nearby on Christmas Eve 1888, and purchased for the sum of £20 by Mr. Fred Pettitt on behalf of the company then erecting the home.

Crouchfield Hotel, demolished 1966.

At Kings Mead School, Belgrave Road, two royal princes - both in their early teens - were among the pupils. Crown Prince Vajiralongkorn of Thailand was visited on more than one occasion by his parents and three sisters, while Prince Ronnie of Buganda had an unexpected call from his father the Kabaka, not long escaped from his homeland following a coup headed by rebel colonel Idi Amin.

In 1967 further housing development took place though this time no existing buildings had to be demolished to make room. Homes were erected on hitherto open land near the sea at Splash Point, thus adding the names of Cliff Close and Cliff Gardens to the fast-filling vacant areas on the local map.

On the same side of town, at the extreme southern end of Southdown Road, Seaford Head Golf Club set their new clubhouse, headquarters and shop. Some

Bainbridge Close, built on the site of Bainbridge Home.

excellent tournaments have since been played, many leading golfers have visited and the course has been sympathetically maintained and up-dated as conditions dictate. The Club's former Chyngton Road premises survived as an hotel and country club till demolition in 1988, after which new homes were built on the site.

A major fire devastated the Golden Galleon Restaurant, overlooking Exceat Bridge as it crosses the Cuckmere. Re-built and since expanded, it gained in popularity and acquired its own brewery alongside. A happy event at the beginning of 1969 was the forging of links with namesake

Surrey Convalescent Home.

Seaford, Long Island, New York State, founded in 1643 by Captain John Seaman who purchased land from the Messapequa Indians and created a settlement named after his Sussex home town. There were still people with that surname living on Long Island, though here it had over the centuries been changed to Simmons.

In April 1969 members of Seaford's Evangelical Free Church, led by pastor Terry Virgo, moved into their first purpose-built church, after five years of raising the £10,000 needed. Earlier services had been held in the "Tin Tabernacle", a former army hut in Upper Belgrave Road.

In 1969 a new police station opened in purpose-built premises on the corner of Church Street and West Street on a site which had lain empty since bombing in the Second World War. Including garages and parking space, the station occupies an area where once stood shops and cottages, among them Chelsea Terrace and Mareesh House. The town's first police force was in a thatched cottage

Cliff Close.

Interior of The Golden Galleon, Exceat.

*Badge of Seaford, Long Island,
New York State, U.S.A.*

Clinton Place, looking west, with bus stop/shelter outside United Reformed Church.

in Upper High Street, east corner of Crouch Lane. From 1896 for more than seventy years the local constabulary operated from No. 2 Chichester Road, with the sergeant's house alongside.

One officer who did not have to make the move was Detective Constable White, who had retired in 1960 after 37 years' police service. Many were his adventures tracking and arresting criminals, uncovering caches of stolen property and coping with war-time problems caused by the presence of so many troops in the area.

Other familiar sights that "went missing" during the 1960s included the closure and eventual demolition of the Splash Point Hotel on the lower cliff; a major chalk fall prompted a decision to re-site the public footpath some way further in from the cliff edge, necessitating the compulsory purchase of the hotel. The figurehead from the Peruvian shipwreck in 1899, rather the worse for wear, was "adopted" by the children of Chyngton Primary School, Millberg Road, who undertook to refurbish her and then put her on display near the front entrance to the school premises. For many years the Southdown bus stops had been in Clinton Place, with the west-going one immediately outside the bus office, where there was an information desk and left-luggage and parcels collection point. At holiday times, the home-going queue for the Brighton bus could cause serious bottlenecks on the narrow pavement; eventually both bus stops were re-sited in the much wider Sutton Park Road.

Chyngton C.P.S. refurbished figurehead.

THE SEVENTIES PROSPERITY AND EXPANSION

In spite of development and modernisation on all sides, the decade began in Seaford with backward glances.

Display of clothing, "A Seaford Kaleidoscope".

On 10th October 1970, "A Seaford Kaleidoscope", an exhibition and slide show, were put on at the Downs Hall. With illustrated talks and displays of clothing, furniture, weapons and other items typical of the eighteenth century, keen local historians re-created a day in the life of old Seaford. Exhibits were borrowed from museums and friends, and included twenty old photographs from Kodak.

During the day five hundred people attended, and a total of £70 was raised with which the original home of Seaford Museum - a caravan - was purchased. Fitted out with archive material, it would be towed to likely spots such as the sea-front or, say, a sports day or similar public event, with the three founders of the Museum, Joan and Ken Astell and Charles Rose, in attendance.

Seaford Museum caravan near Martello Tower.

One of the first tasks they and their supporters undertook was clearing rubbish that had accumulated in and around that hitherto undervalued piece of

Seaford heritage, the crypt. Not since historian M.A. Lower wrote about the building more than a century before - till the Museum took an interest - had anyone realised its historic value. When archaeologists visited Seaford six years later to investigate a possible medieval site opposite the parish church, they identified the crypt as a thirteenth-century vaulted undercroft of a house "likely to have been occupied by a wealthy merchant". A small notice to this effect was fixed to the exterior flint wall, but it disappeared soon afterwards. The building remained unvisited for

(L - R) Charles Rose, Ken Astell, Museum caravan interior.

another eighteen years, except for an occasional guided viewing, conducted by Museum members.

Following the closure of The Downs School and Lewes District Council moving into the main premises, the separate building known as The Library became the headquarters of the Downs Day Club for the Elderly, with a croquet lawn and a terrace which made an ideal stage for open-air theatricals. The clubhouse has been extended several times since.

The Downs Day Club Drama Group: Mrs. Edith Tietjen as Queen Catherine Parr, Mr. Bill Perkins as King Henry VIII in old age.

Also in 1970 Seaford Lifeguards was founded, establishing a service to the community which many never need to call upon, though all are reassured to know of its existence. Renowned for its tricky currents, unexpected giant waves and the wash from cross-channel ferries, Seaford Bay must always be treated with respect by those disporting themselves in or on its waters.

The Downs Day Club: building of extension.

From the sea-front it was possible to witness work in progress near Newhaven harbour, as a new Royal Sovereign lightship was built. On 15th June 1970 the 4000-ton construction was towed across Seaford Bay to its station eight miles off Beachy Head.

At 6.30 pm on Sunday 18th October that same year Seaford's Roman Catholic community gathered to welcome their Bishop, the Right Reverend David Cashman, S.T.L. at the church of St. Thomas More. The occasion was the consecration of the altar and the official opening of the new extension, which had been included in architect J. O'Hanlon Hughes' original drawing, showing the church "as it will be when completed". It would be a further fourteen years before the building of the final section, the church hall.

Royal Sovereign Lightship, Seaford Bay.

Following major alterations at the church of St. Peter the apostle, East Blatchington, and the re-siting of pews, pulpit, organ, font and choir stalls, in 1970 a new altar of plain stone was installed, in memory of churchwarden Robert Hall. The church stands on a site where Roman remains were found during excavations in 1860. Among graves in the churchyard are those of Robert Lambe, a local farmer on whose land much of Claremont Road was built in 1879, as an inland by-pass away from the eroded seaside route to the west. Others buried here are Dr. William Tyler Smith who came to Seaford in 1857 intending to develop it into "a second Brighton", Thomas Anstey Guthrie who, as F. Anstey, wrote a popular Victorian novel "Vice Versa", and a number of soldiers from the eighteenth-century Blatchington Barracks, and their families.

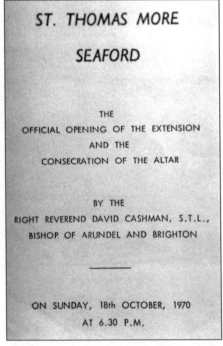

ST. THOMAS MORE

SEAFORD

THE
OFFICIAL OPENING OF THE EXTENSION
AND THE
CONSECRATION OF THE ALTAR

BY THE
RIGHT REVEREND DAVID CASHMAN, S.T.L.,
BISHOP. OF ARUNDEL AND BRIGHTON

———

ON SUNDAY, 18th OCTOBER, 1970
AT 6.30 P.M.

Announcement of visit to St. Thomas More Church by the Bishop of Arundel and Brighton.

New estates were developed on the large areas of land released for building by further closures of local preparatory and boarding schools, some of these being commemorated in the names of new roads (Stoke Manor, Kings Mead, Chesterton). The influx of occupants of the houses built was reflected in the 1971 census, which revealed Seaford's population standing at 16,226, greater than that of the county town of Lewes. Many of these new Seaforders might be termed "commuter families", the wage-earners travelling by road or rail to work in London, Gatwick or Croydon, with the benefit of sea and countryside to be had at weekends.

In October 1971, clearance began of a site at the junction of Belgrave Road and Westdown Road, where a new church for Seaford's Baptist congregation would eventually stand. Their original church was founded in 1889 in a "tin chapel" on the

Grave of Robert Lambe, Blatchington Church graveyard.

north-east corner of High Street and South Street, on ground formerly part of Mrs. Gorringe's garden. After eleven years the congregation moved to purpose-built premises in Broad Street where they stayed till March 1972 after which the church and hall were demolished. For a while Broad Street shoppers could see clear through to the east wall of St. Leonard's graveyard, and an unusual end-on view of the parish church itself.

The Broad Street site (No. 29A) was then developed with "a modern walk-round store" for Boots the Chemist. The original tin chapel survived a further thirty years till demolished and replaced in 2003 by a block of town houses. Till the Belgrave Road church was ready, the Baptist congregation met in St. John's Hall, Wilmington Road.

On the evening of Wednesday 2nd February 1972, the 435-ton German coaster *Walter Richter* (Captain Meyer and six crew) with a cargo of

Grave of soldier from Blatchington Barracks.

View of Seaford Parish Church from Broad Street.

beechwood was driven ashore opposite the ruins of Tide Mills village, in a gale. Valiant work was done by coastguards, lifeboatmen, police and lifeguards in

saving the stranded seamen; onlookers who had gathered on the beach helped launch the rocket-line carrying the breeches buoy to the stricken vessel. Four men had been safely brought ashore when the *Walter Richter's* end of the line jammed. Without hesitation, lifeguard captain Peter Lewis dashed into the boiling sea and, after a struggle, managed to get aboard and release the mechanism and the rescue was completed.

It was anticipated that the coaster would be re-floated within a few high tides, but it was in fact four weeks - during which she suffered damage with every rough sea

German coaster Walter Richter aground near Tide Mills.

- before Newhaven's Metrec tug "Mallard", working in conjunction with a shore-based winch, succeeded where other salvage vessels had failed. In the time the *Walter Richter* sat on the beach she became quite a tourist attraction and is still vividly remembered by those who saw her over thirty years ago.

Seaford Young Musicians at West House.

Formed in 1973, Seaford Young Musicians had its first headquarters at West House, closely linked with fellow-residents, Seaford Museum. Directed by Mrs. Pat White (who transcribed music for any and every instrument brought along), by 1991 they had one hundred and ten members of various ages and degrees of musicianship. Sadly, times changed and other musical outlets became available; in 2000 SYM closed down, having had in its time some 650 young people aged between 7 and 17 (including some "second generation") through its hands, plus a number of adult helpers. The group gave two concerts a year, every current member taking part, no matter what their instrument or experience.

Seaford Public Library, from its one-room origins behind the Baptist Church in Broad Street (see p.37), had moved next door to the gas show-rooms in Sutton Park Road in April 1947. It expanded into the vacated show-rooms in the mid-1960s and, in 1973, became only the second library in the county to adopt computer registration. At the time of writing the Friends of Seaford Library and other agencies are agitating most urgently for new or enlarged premises for this popular and hard-pressed facility.

Army Cadets entrain for Annual Camp on the Isle of Man (picture courtesy of the Argus).

In August 1973, boys of the Seaford detachment of the Army Cadet Force went off to Sussex annual camp on the Isle of Man, which was still in shock from the effects of a major fire at the £2m Summerland entertainment complex in Douglas, which left thirty dead and over eighty injured. The cadets had the opportunity to show their sympathy when invited to take part in a carnival parade through the streets of Douglas, where they moved among the spectators with plastic buckets, filled time and again with cash donations to help the victims.

Towards the end of that year, the country was put in an official state of emergency. An overtime ban by miners, power workers and railwaymen, together with cuts in public spending and financial crises with a rise in the bank rate, all intensified by the outbreak of the Arab-Israeli war, led to "the gravest situation by far since the end of the war" (1945). A speed limit of 50 mph on roads was imposed in order to conserve fuel, and all television channels closed down at 10.30 pm. One strange result was that, for the first time ever, Sunday (daylight) play was permitted for professional football matches.

Pilgrimage to the Holy Land.

In October 1973, five members of St. Luke's Church, Chyngton, joined a group led by Bishop Stanley Betts, Dean of Rochester, on a pilgrimage to the Holy Land "in the steps of our Lord". Security throughout their fourteen-day visit was fierce, with many screenings and "friskings", but anything was worth the awesome moments they experienced in seeing places hitherto known only through Bible references. At the Dome of the Rock, they were in a building venerated equally by Christians, Jews and Moslems: "We stayed a short while there, with our own silent thoughts and prayers". The party made three attempts to visit Jericho but each time were turned back by soldiers, though they were allowed to drive to the Golan Heights where they saw the source of the river Jordan.

As already mentioned (see p. 15), Seaford Urban District Council came to an end only twenty two years after its grant of arms: in 1974, through the re-organisation of local government, Seaford came under the control of Lewes District Council, with only a subcommittee representing our town - a long drop from the self-governing Cinque Port member of 150 years before, with its own two Parliamentary representatives, its own court, its own powers of life or death.

On 23rd July 1974, the Rt. Hon. William Whitelaw, C.H., M.C., D.L. M.P., Chairman of the Conservative Party, performed the opening ceremony of the new Seaford & District Constitutional Club building, Crouch Lane, on the site of the Crouchfield Hotel.

Seaford & District Constitutional Club, Crouch Lane.

During her time as Conservative Minister for Education in the mid-1970s, Mrs. Margaret Thatcher addressed a meeting at the Downs Hall, on the subject of school zoning - children being allocated to the schools closest to their homes. Hospitality

West House, early home of Seaford Museum.

was provided at a house in Saxon Lane which for several years from 1979, when Mrs. Thatcher became Prime Minister, displayed in the dining area a small plaque commemorating her visit. On change of ownership of the premises, the plaque was removed.

By 1975, Seaford Museum had outgrown its caravan and was established in West House, on the corner of Steyne Road and Pelham Road (believed to have been the harbourmaster's house in Cinque Ports days). The building, in spite of its age and history, was earmarked for demolition whenever a proposed ring road should be made; in the meantime, though all mains services were off, the local authority allowed the Museum to move in. Thus, on 14th November 1975, local historians were able to gather to hear accounts of what took place "in this very room, on this very night, one hundred years ago": it was the centenary of the great storm, when the room was filled to the ceiling with flood water of such force that it tore wallpaper from the walls and dislodged a whole mantelpiece. By the light of lanterns and candles, members read out eye-witness reports to a suitably stunned audience.

This was the year when the town suffered yet another indignity, when the railway line from Newhaven, double-tracked since 1904, was "singled", thus making our station technically a siding once again. Its long platforms remained as a reminder of the station's days of glory serving volunteer soldiers bringing their horses for manoeuvres on the downs, boarding school children arriving and departing, and holiday makers, convalescents and hikers seeking quiet, sunshine and clear air.

A fair example of "Sussex won't be druv" occurred in March 1975 when Mr. Lou Scharer, proprietor of Kemp's Garage, Steyne Road, after some differences of opinion with the Inland Revenue, paid the sum of £471.62 by cheque, written on a piece of paving stone.

The Esplanade Hotel, background for a sea-front parade.

The sea-front Esplanade Hotel, built in 1891 (with the five-storey west wing added three years later) as the crowning glory of the developers' plans for Seaford to rival Brighton, never recovered from the change in fashions both before and after the Second World War. By the 1960s, some of its busiest times were the Sunday luncheons served to visiting parents, bringing their sons and daughters out for the day from their nearby boarding schools. Some local organisations continued to hold annual dinners and other social occasions at the hotel, and location shots for one or two feature films were made

The Esplanade Hotel, destroyed by fire.

there, but the building grew shabby and forlorn - a far cry from the establishment that welcomed King Edward VII (plus pet terrier Caesar) in 1905.

Squatters appeared to have taken over the empty building by 1976, when fire broke out and brought the end of a once grand hotel. From time to time thereafter planning applications were made for building blocks of flats, three-bedroomed houses and the like, but the site stood empty till 1987 when Mallett Close, named in memory of a brave Victorian coastguard, was built.

Farther west along the sea-front, the Eversley Hotel was still in business. A bill of fare from 1977 has survived:

Rainbow trout	£1.75
Rump steak	1.75
Mixed grill	1.85
Gammon & pineapple	1.55
Chicken Kiev	1.85
Salmon steak	1.75
Soup of the day	20p
Sweets	25p - 45p
Beaujolais	2.60 per bottle
Spanish sauterne	40p per glass
Champagne	6.50 per bottle

Periodically the sea-front properties were lashed by storms and high seas; many windows were permanently protected with wire netting and it was a common sight to see waves breaking over the rooftops. Following gales in 1978, it was proposed to spend £ 246,000 in re-furbishing Nos. 2 - 8, property of the District Council who, two years earlier, had sought approval to demolish them;

Rough seas at the Martello Tower.

this was rejected by the Department of the Environment.

The long hot summer of 1976 will be remembered by local archaeology enthusiasts as the time they were able to dirty their hands and damage their backs in the interests of historical accuracy. For generations it had been believed that relics of a western wing of the parish church lay beneath the surface where Nos. 39 - 47 Church Street had stood. When the survivors of these old buildings were demolished, and before the area was re-developed as the new main Post Office, a team of professional archaeologists, with local volunteers helping, had the opportunity to excavate the site. Only traces of domestic occupation were found: several wells yielded pottery shards and broken vessels, and animal bones from medieval times.

Large areas of building land had been released by the closure of schools and convalescent homes in the sixties, with corresponding increases in numbers of residences and of

Site of archaeological dig, Church Street, 1976.

population. In addition to those already mentioned, Ladycross - the Roman Catholic boys' school in Eastbourne Road since 1909 - fell to the demolition hammer nearly seventy years later. The site was re-developed as Badgers Close; at the time of writing, the brick pillars that once guarded the school entrance still stand. It was the proud record of Ladycross that more than 350 former

Building starts on the new Post Office, on the same site.

pupils fought in the First World War.

1977 marked Her Majesty the Queen's silver jubilee; Seaford celebrated with a programme of events at the Salts Recreation Ground and advertisers in the souvenir brochure entered into the spirit of the occasion.

In the same year, despite efforts to save it for its unique contents, a house in Grosvenor Road was demolished. In 1921, Pullman sleeping cars from the Victorian Inverness to Glasgow night train had been towed by tractor from storage in Brighton and built into the property, interior doors and marquetry panels with an owl motif being visible therein for more than half a century.

The condition of the 170-year-old Martello Tower No. 74, built overlooking Seaford Bay to defend our shores in the event of cross-channel invasion, was giving cause for concern to its owners, Lewes District Council. A major refurbishment was carried out, with the removal from above the gun platform of the apartment added in 1922, installation of a new wooden floor at street level, replacement of the curving stairway leading to the lowest level, and other work to restore the venerable old building to its original design, as nearly as modern safety regulations would allow.

The management of Seaford Museum were the successful applicants for the tenancy on completion of the work, and the day came when Lewes District Council Chairman Cllr. Mrs. Shirley Whitely performed the opening

Advertisement in brochure of celebration of H.M. the Queen's silver jubilee.

First displays of Seaford Museum in the Martello Tower.

ceremony on 12th April, 1979.

In July of the same year in Crouch Lane, Seaford House - the third of that name on the same site - was opened as sheltered accommodation for the elderly. Charles Rose Ellis (Baron Seaford), George Canning (Prime Minister while M.P. for Seaford) and Alfred, Lord Tennyson (Poet Laureate 1850 - 92) were among celebrities who had resided in the first house, pulled down and replaced in about 1860.

The third Seaford House, Crouch Lane.

On 11th March 1973 Seaford lost one of its stalwarts with the death of Colonel Rex Anthony Edward Hillman, T.D. Educated at Southdown School, Firle Road, Seaford, and Malvern College, in 1920 he was articled to his father's legal firm in Lewes.

He joined the 5th Battalion Royal Sussex Regiment Territorial Army; in the 1926 General Strike his duty was guarding the bridge at Beddingham.

During a life of service to the town he was for ten years (till the outbreak of the Second World War) a member of Seaford Urban District Council, and its chairman in 1934.

As a captain on active service in WW2 he fought at El Alamein, rising to command a PAIFORCE* camp for two years, and thence to the Judge Advocates Department in Baghdad.

Post-war, his concerns included: solicitor and clerk to Newhaven and Seaford Sea Defence Commissioners, chairman of National Insurance tribunals and of Blatchington Court School for the partially sighted, president Royal Sussex Old Comrades, and president for 21 years of Seaford British Legion. Local lawn tennis, golf, cricket and hockey groups and the Union Club all received his active support, and he was president of several of these.

In 52 years with the family firm of solicitors he rose to become senior partner and was still serving as a consultant at his death. I am proud to have been employed in the Seaford office for a small part of that time by this true gentleman of the old school; it was for me an honour and a pleasure.

* Persia and Iraq Force (a camp for political internees at Sultanbad).

The Late Colonel R. A. E. Hillman, T.D.

THE EIGHTIES
DEVASTATION
AND
RESTORATION

For a number of years the question of a separate Seaford Council had been discussed and deferred: matters such as the issue of bus passes (which needed to be ratified by a town authority, which Seaford did not have) were involved. In 1980 the town's first-ever referendum was held on the subject, and it was rejected. The issue was not to be resolved for a further fifteen years.

Blatchington Pond.

Until the early twentieth century Blatchington Pond (earliest known record 1645) complemented on the diagonally opposite corner the smaller rectangular Lily Pond, but this had been drained and premises erected, to be occupied in turn by Redcourts Country Club and the Elm Court Youth Club. Thereafter the depth, area and status of the surviving pond varied greatly, according to weather conditions and public opinion. When in the late 1970s East Blatchington was designated a Conservation Area, a group of enthusiasts raised some £2,000 for the restoration of the pond. From 1980 on, with expert advice and help (fully described in a leaflet available from the Tourist Information Centre) tremendous changes for the better have taken place, attracting a wide range of resident and visiting wildlife.

In 1980 and 1981, discussions and visits to and fro were held with towns in France and West Germany, looking towards some official "twinning". An early event was held jointly with representatives of Seaford and Bönningstedt one Saturday morning at Corsica Hall, with entertainment by Seaford Silver Band, and discussions moved on till 19th May 1984, when documents were signed confirming the official link, since when many exchange visits have taken place: a stretch of our promenade was given the name of our "Twin" in honour of the accord.

"A popular event in pre-war days" and started up again in 1950 when the dust from the Second World War had settled, Seaford's annual Games Tourney was soon back in its stride, with 300 entrants for the Children's Sports in 1951

Cllr. Miss Renee Oeters inaugurates the ladies' bowling competition.

... and 500 in 1976. For a number of years from 1977 the Tourney was organized by the local Chamber of Commerce and comprised tennis, golf, cricket, stoolball, sailing, bowls and children's sports, the last always held on a Wednesday afternoon (then recognised as "half-day closing" - shopkeeping members of the Chamber were therefore free to assist). On 28th July 1980, Miss Renee Oeters inaugurated the ladies' bowls competition at the Crouch Bowling Club, supported by Mr. John Berry, President of Seaford Chamber of Commerce, and Mrs. Berry, and officials of the Club.

That same year, Pilgrims School in Firle Road was honoured by a second visit from its patron, H.R.H. Princess Margaret. In 1955 she had opened the school for the Invalid Children's Association for young sufferers with asthmatic conditions, and returned to celebrate its silver jubilee.

Yet another boarding school shut down: after more than fifty years at premises in Firle Road, with headmasters Mr. Seagrove and Mr. Hackett increasing the number of boys to 95 in 1947, Normansal closed. Sports master both before and after the Second

Mr. Arthur Bartlett (sports master) and boys of Normansal School.

Mme. Genevieve Le Halle (right) and the author on the gun platform, Martello Tower No. 74.

World War was Mr. Arthur Bartlett; he also taught boxing at St. Peter's prep school, and later at the local boys' Club. Chalvington School succeeded Normansal in Firle Road. From 1909 till 1929, the same site had been occupied by Lexden School, remembered today in nearby street names.

The official census taken in 1981 produced a total population in Seaford of 17,785. In that year several tours of the Martello Tower Museum were arranged for French groups: the one on 16th April was unusual in that there were only two visitors, M. and Mme. Guy Le Halle. Guy wished to research our Tower No. 74 for his forthcoming book "Les Fortifications".

The Royal British Legion celebrated its diamond jubilee in 1981, marking sixty years of work in aid of the ex-service community throughout the country. Seaford branch staged a spectacular event at the Salts Recreation Ground, with a grand parade and a full programme with something for everyone.

For the second year in succession there was a rare pre-Christmas fall of snow, this time on Tuesday, 8th December; in 1980, my diary recorded, there was a slight flurry at 2.30 pm on Friday, 28th November.

1982 was designated by National Heritage as Maritime Year. Seaford Museum's contribution included an exhibition and booklet covering two hundred years of shipwrecks in the bay, and an entertainment in the Claremont Hall on 10th December. Among items enjoyed was a hornpipe danced by members of the Junior Group (wearing authentic sailor collars from the Museum collection) and a verbatim re-enactment of presentations made in 1870

Seaford Museum's Maritime evening: Junior Group hornpipe/re-enactment of Richard Mallett presentation (standing, l-r: Mr. Ernest Teitjen, Mr. Peter White).

to the gallant coastguard Richard Mallett for his life-saving feats when the French brig Seraphin ran aground opposite The Causeway in a fierce gale.

In spite of rumours in the 1960s that HRH Prince Charles might become a pupil there, St. Peter's School, founded in Alfriston Road in 1904, suffered like so many others in the area from the changing approaches to education, and to boarding schools in particular. In 1982, shortly after one of its most distinguished former pupils, Colonel "H" Jones, was posthumously awarded the Victoria Cross for

St. Peter's School: the main building/the chapel.

his actions at the battle of Goose Green in the Falklands War, St. Peter's closed. Consequently, great interest resulted in an auction of contents; Seaford Museum now displays the school's memorial board and a stained glass window. (Another former pupil was Anthony Blunt, once art adviser to HM the Queen, unmasked as a member of the Burgess/Maclean spy ring and stripped of his honours).

On 1st August 1982 Father William Guinane, parish priest of St. Thomas More Church, died after some twenty years' service to Seaford's Catholic community. Among his first undertakings was the extension of the church, begun in 1935. He was succeeded in 1980 by Father Kenneth McCarthy, under whose guidance the splendid Parish Hall (where a number of local groups meet) was built in 1984, replacing the wooden building that had been a gift of the Dutton family.

Gravestone of Fr. William Guinane, Alfriston Road cemetery.

Replacement of cannon, Martello Tower: preliminary discussions/completed cannon.

At the beginning of the decade, Lewes District Council as owners of the Martello Tower were in discussion with Portsmouth Corporation about the permanent loan of a cannon, to replace the one removed from the tower roof in 1882. In September 1980 representatives of the District Council and the Museum spent a day at a Gosport Royal Navy shore establishment, where a timber gun carriage was to be designed and built. All plans were shelved on the outbreak of the Falklands War in 1982; the carriage was eventually completed and installed by workers from the Manpower Service Commission; the complete cannon unit continues to be the exterior focal point of the Tower.

Seaford Museum made a jolly start to 1984 with a "Victorian Evening" on 28th January at the Claremont Hall. Entertainers, guests, hosts and hostesses dressed in appropriate costumes, played cards and old-fashioned table games, before the presentation of *The House on the Beach*. This was a free adaptation of the short novel by George Meredith, who lived in Seaford 1856/7, and is believed to have had the town in mind as its setting.

An additional feature of the 1984 Games Tourney was a session of Short Tennis at the club in Belgrave Road, attended by a number of aspiring young athletes. No-one went home empty-handed: prizes ranged from medals and miniature cups to bottles of lemonade.

In 1985 occurred the death of popular entertainer Dickie Henderson, who had been educated at Seaford's Annecy Convent in Sutton Avenue. His father was a successful music hall comic, also Dickie Henderson, so for some years son Dickie added "Junior" to his billing. An early American film role in an adaptation of Noel Coward's *Cavalcade* left him with a pleasant mid-Atlantic

The cast of "The House on the Beach" (reproduced by kind permission of the Sussex Express & County Herald).

Presentation of prizes to all who took part in the Short Tennis event.

accent. At the height of his success he appeared in more than one hundred episodes of his own television show, and starred in Eastbourne pantomimes for a number of years.

Chyngton Methodist Church in Millberg Road had been established there in 1955 by members of the Steyne Road sister church who saw a need in the newly-developed area of Seaford; by the 1980s, it had grown so much that an extension to the original building was required.

Little did British Gas workers David Brett and Frank Blackford, digging a trench in Upper High Street for pipe re-laying in December 1986, realise they were about to become hot news in the archaeological world. Outside No. 34, they came upon a cache of fifteen worked flint axeheads, dated by experts as five thousand years old. A halt was called and East Sussex County Council archaeologist Dr. Andrew Woodcock summoned from Lewes. With so many stones

Entertainer Dickie Henderson, former Annecy pupil.

grouped together, it was thought to be the largest single find of such flints in the south. One suggestion at the time was that they may have been a Neolithic flint-knappers' "window display"!

To create additional exhibition space at the Martello Tower, Museum members launched a "Buy a Brick" campaign, raising funds to build an enclosing wall at each end of the roofed-in part of the dry moat area. A total of £1070.50 (the equivalent of 4283 "bricks") resulted from the first of a series of prize draws, the winning ticket being drawn on Wednesday 2nd July 1986 by Radio Brighton celebrity David Arscott, an enthusiastic supporter of the Museum. Members' claim to have "the museum with hidden depths" came abundantly true that day.

Seventeen days later, on Saturday 19th July, Sainsbury's store in Broad Street closed its doors for

Dr. Andrew Woodcock with 5000-year-old flint axe-heads.

the last time, after almost fifty years as one of the town's leading grocers and butchers. A new bus route C.10 (Sutton Park Road to Lewes Road, Brighton) offered free transport along the coast road each Tuesday, Thursday and Friday, outward journey leaving Seaford at 9.25 am, back at 5.30 pm, so that customers could continue to support Sainsbury's at the Brighton store.

In the same year the Ritz cinema on the corner of Pelham Road and Dane Road - a sad shadow of its former glamorous self, opened in 1936 - was demolished to make way for a Safeway store; across the road, the old Southdown bus garage, later the Sea Defence depot, suffered a similar fate, as the new health centre rose from the

David Arscott draws winning ticket in "Buy a Brick" event at Seaford Museum.

rubble. The St. Crispians estate was built on the site of the railway goods yard, and Mallett Close - named in memory of the Victorian coastguard hero - took the place of the Esplanade Hotel, on the eastern corner of the sea-front and The Causeway.

From time to time throughout this book, reference has been made to the schemes put forward to save and improve the sea defences of Seaford's 2½ mile coastline, against the forces of the Channel.

An exhibition had been mounted at the Little Theatre, Steyne Road, where residents could see and discuss with experts three broad suggestions for such a rescue. The ideas were (1) to erect concrete groynes in place of existing wooden ones (2) to build an artificial "atoll" in the bay, to divide the direction of the waves and diminish their force (3) to raise the height of the shingle beach, burying all existing groynes; to counteract the resulting build-up of shingle driven by the current, periodically heavy vehicles would transport the excess back to its original position.

The third scheme, costing £9 million, was chosen and work began in the spring of 1987. A 439-ft. dredger, the *Barent Zanen* became a familiar sight, anchored in the bay day and night, reminding some local historians of older residents' memories: "on stormy evenings long ago, the bay would give shelter to many ships; with their lamps aglow, it seemed like another town out there". Millions of tons of shingle - brought by barges plying to and from the Owers Bank (off Littlehampton) - were mixed with water and sprayed through a giant pipeline, to be flattened by bulldozers, till a mile-long new beach, level with the esplanade and devoid of any groyne or other obstacle, was created.

Within hours of completion of the work, the worst storm to hit our coast for many a year - the hurricane of 16th-17th October 1987 - drove the shingle onto the promenade and into great mounds on the beach. The "morning after" scene suggested the re-charging work of many months might never have been carried

Stages in the demolition of Ritz Cinema and building of Safeway store.

Site ready for redevelopment as Health Centre, Dane Road.

out: had that been the case, the whole unprotected sea-wall would have collapsed, with stormwater flooding the lower levels of the town. Thus, the re-charging scheme had saved us. Work began immediately to restore the shingle, and subsequently the defences have behaved as suggested in plan (3). Inland, on that

Aftermath of rough seas: shingle thrown up on seafront opposite Salts Recreation Ground.

horrific October night, as a result of the excessively strong winds, trees were uprooted and tiles torn from roofs, fences flattened, garden plants and bushes ripped from the earth. Caravans were overturned, the roof of the Baptist Church in Belgrave Road destroyed, and public services disrupted. The most disastrous storm for more than a century continues to this day to be the landmark date from which other events are calculated. A cheery sight after so much destruction around the town centre was the new painting by Keith Wallace on the west-facing wall of the Rolf brothers' wet fish shop, depicting the "crew" at sea, with a distant view of the town behind them.

The theme of Seaford Festival of the Arts in 1988 was "Tudor Times" - an important era for the town, with King Henry VIII granting its first charter (though it had been a part of the Cinque Ports system since the thirteenth century, if not earlier), the building of the Town Hall in South Street, and the Spanish Armada sailing hotly pursued by Queen Elizabeth I's fleet, but out of sight from our shores. Festival items included the Rosemary Jayne Dancers in *The Six Wives of Henry*, the Young Drama Group's presentation of *Elizabethan Ruffle*, and the Museum's exhibition and illustrated talk *Tudor Seaford*.

Seaford Head Golf Club's former headquarters in Chyngton Road were sold

for redevelopment, and on Sunday 25th September guests were invited to the Manor House at Bishopstone to celebrate its three-hundredth birthday. The building bears over the front door the date 1688 and initials "T*P" referring to Thomas, 1st Baron Pelham of Laughton. It was here in

Beach re-charging operations.

Resulting beach and restoring shingle.

1761 that another Thomas Pelham, Duke of Newcastle, conceived the idea of harnessing the tidal waters of the river Ouse to work a flour mill.

On Friday 23rd December the Belgian trawler *White Horse* got into difficulties, ran aground at The Buckle and stuck there for several days, providing an extra point of interest for

The hurricane: trees uprooted, gas pipe fractured.

families out on the traditional post-Christmas-dinner sea-front rambles. There were some dramatic moments when over-strained hawsers, intended to draw the vessel out into deep water, snapped and whipped back towards the spectators. Tugs from Newhaven (with their seasonal fir trees lashed to the masts in time-honoured local manner) eventually pulled her clear.

After several years languishing at the Museum, the figurehead of the Peruvian, wrecked on Seaford beach in 1899, at last received the "beauty treatment" she deserved, with a full restoration and painting in carefully-researched authentic colours by David Taylor, who then gave an illustrated talk about his work to fellow Museum members.

Messrs. Rolf's mural by Keith Wallace.

One night in June 1989, neighbours in South Street were evacuated from their homes as fire raged through the centuries-old Town Hall, at the time in use as headquarters of the local St. John Ambulance Brigade. The little building had withstood riots, a break-out from its dungeon, and numerous demonstrations at unpopular announcements of election results; on one occasion it was so badly damaged that demolition was seriously considered. Now, in the cold light of morning, it stood with scorched rafters and ruined interior, a sad and sorry sight, its fate undecided.

Those who feared the remains of the building might have to be taken down were reassured when repair work was put in hand: in fact, so sympathetic was the restoration that some older features (never witnessed by present generations but only read about in

Demolition of Seaford Head Hotel (formerly Seaford Head Golf Club H.Q.)

history books) were included. In May, 1990, the retiring Chairman of Lewes District Council, Group Captain John Palmer, accompanied by Mrs. Vera Palmer, marked the completion of the work by unveiling a bronze plaque detailing the history of the building. A Seaford resident, he had chosen the plaque as his traditional leaving gift to the town. The hall has since been used as a "Drop In" coffee shop (now with computer facilities for all) and it is once more the busy centre of activity our ancestors knew centuries ago, with electors, bailiffs and jurats frequenting it in the old Corporation days when the town followed its Cinque Ports ways.

Belgian trawler 'White Horse' stranded at The Buckle.

Fire damage, Old Town Hall, South Street.

Retiring Chairman of Lewes District Council, Group Captain John Palmer, unveils commemorative plaque, Old Town Hall.

Renovated 'Peruvian' figurehead.

THE NINETIES COMMEMORATION AND MILLENNIUM

As yet, no documentary proof has been found precisely dating the town church, known to us as the parish church of St. Leonard, Seaford, but experts in ecclesiastical architecture had compared St. Leonard's with other early Norman churches, and put its date at 1090. Thus, great celebrations were planned to coincide with the opening of the last decade of the twentieth century, including the publication of an up-dated edition of *The Parish Church of St. Leonard', Seaford* by Dr. J. G. Taylor.

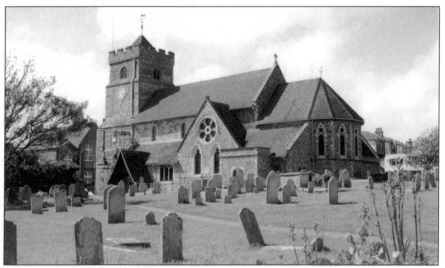

Parish Church of St. Leonard from south-east.

The population of the town, as recorded in the 1991 census, was 20,933, a four-fold increase in the number for 1921 and eleven times the total a century earlier.

The Festival of the Arts (29th June - 13th July that year) included an evening of readings by celebrated actor and writer David Kossoff, local players in an adaptation of Louisa M. Alcott's *Little Women*, folk dancing, and concerts by Seaford Silver Band.

For a number of years, Seaford Museum arranged a large-scale fund-raising day in the dry moat of the Martello Tower: typical themes included *Patchwork, Nautical, My Hat!* and *In the Pink* (illustrated); scenes of activity were recorded by long-serving Museum member Mr. George Jakens.

In September 1991 the Museum arranged a visit by "owl-man" Julian Ford, who brought a number of his beautiful birds to the Barn Theatre. He talked about (and to) them, demonstrated their flight, and encouraged members of his audience to befriend

Mr. David Kossoff.

them. One sat on Miss Bartlett's gloved hand for so long that her arm stiffened in the "hold" position, while Mrs. Jill Martin got acquainted with another.

By this time, the County Primary School in Church Street, built in 1878 and extended eleven years later, having suffered storms, enemy air raids and the passage of time, was deemed inadequate for the number

Seaford Museum: "In the Pink" fund-raising day.

of children needing primary education in the town. As a last reunion of former pupils was held, building of a new school was already well under way on land in Belgrave Road. This was the site of a grand house, once the home of Dr.

William Tyler Smith who had endeavoured to make Victorian Seaford into "a second Brighton". His home became a girls' school in 1932 and was eventually Blatchington Court, a school for partially-sighted children. The area cleared by the demolition of the house was sufficient for the modern County Primary school and two new roads - Wilkinson Way and Foster Close - with additional housing.

The name of Councillor Diana Stiles is linked with two public schemes in this decade: in 1993, Lower and Upper High Streets were enhanced by rebuilding the pavements with brickwork and installing Victorian-style lamp standards; ten years on, the mellow evening colouring is still appreciated. To an historian, it calls to mind some of the dramatic events that occurred here, silently witnessed by buildings still standing on either side of the

Seaford Museum: Mr. George Jakens filming the above.

narrow old road. Cllr. Stiles was also instrumental in the development of the Church Street area called locally "The Crypt". Now known to be Seaford's oldest surviving secular edifice, the box-like flint-walled building had for years received scant care or attention, save only from the likes of Mr. M. A. Lower and Mr. W. R. Wynter, writing almost a century ago, and members of Seaford Museum in the 1970s.

An imaginative scheme to erect a modern

Mrs. Jill Martin with Julian Ford and feathered friend.

Enhancement of the High Street: Tony Wilson, Jim Billings & Peter Caiser. Enhancement of the High Street: the result.

The Crypt Gallery.

masonry "shell" to enclose the entire original, with internal space between for exhibitions and lectures, came true in 1994; today the Crypt Gallery is in frequent use for art, craft and photographic displays and a variety of meetings and small social gatherings.

Visit of Footsbarn Travelling Theatre.

In July 1993, as part of Brighton Festival, the members of Footsbarn Travelling Theatre set up their giant tent and mobile village, complete with school, in Martello Fields behind the Museum. With masks, original music, puppets, slapstick and quick-change costume, they presented their own interpretation of Shakespeare's *Romeo and Juliet*. The full company of thirty two was drawn from nine countries.

A year later, the Museum's special exhibition featured the work of local

blacksmiths and farriers, with items and explanations from Mr. F. Haynes of Frank's Forge. These included the story of the hen blackbird that lived for several years in the old Crouch Lane building, anecdotes of earlier smiths and folklore such as the reason for the traditional fringed hems of their leather aprons - when one of them

Museum special exhibition: The Blacksmith & Farrier.

was favoured by God, his jealous rivals slashed at him with knives as he was whisked up to heaven.

TransAtlantic links with the community in Seaford, Long Island, New York State, were maintained by visits from Stanton Behr and Frank Abrami to the Museum and other local features.

November 1994 saw the inauguration of an annual event which, one hopes, will continue as long as the world lasts. Earlier in the year Mr. Bob Baxter, National Chairman of the Canadian Veterans' Association and a resident of Brighton, made enquiries about the possibility that Canadian soldiers from the First World War were buried in Seaford. Although some residents knew there were 191 such graves in the Alfriston Road cemetery (most of them victims of the Spanish 'flu epidemic 1918 - 19, rather than of war wounds or gas attacks), it was news to the veterans, who were soon liaising with Seaford Royal British Legion and me, with the result that an impressively solemn and moving ceremony of remembrance took place at the cemetery. A drive back to town via the site of North Camp and the Parish Church - where the party were able to see the pews, with commemorative brass maple-leaf plaques, given by the Canadians before they left in 1919 - brought us to Legion Headquarters in Claremont Road, where lasting friendships were founded.

Mr. Stanton Behr of Seaford, Long Island, visits the Museum.

Concern had been growing about the fate of the open space off the sea-front known as "the brickfield". Test borings, fencing off and other activities by the owners alerted neighbours to the possibility that this site, valued for its history and for its rare flora and fauna, might be lost through development. A petition with 228 signatures was organised in Spring, 1995; as a result the land was saved by Lewes District Council making a compulsory purchase.

Another happy ending that year was the safe return of Jimbo the parrot, missing for two months from the Pet Love shop in Saxon Lane. As if his trade mark "wolf whistle" did not identify him enough when he was found in Newhaven, DNA testing proved it.

In December, Cradle Hill County Primary School staged *"Joseph and his Amazing Technicolour Dreamcoat"*, while the choir of Seaford C.P.S. (now firmly established in Wilkinson Way) took part in a candlelit concert organised by the

Mr. Bob Baxter, National Chairman, Canadian Veterans' Association, lays their wreath at the first "pilgrimage" to Alfriston Road cemetery.

Rotary Club of Seaford in the Parish Church, with a comprehensive mix of local musicians, from international favourite soprano Felicity Lott, singing two arias from Handel's "Messiah", to flautist Alison Back, trumpeter Michael Bunting, the Silver Quartet led by Gordon Hammel, and accompanist Margaret Darwall-Smith, to carols for everyone with John Baker at the organ, and readings by Seaford Rotarians. Our lovely old church showed at its very best in the mellow candlelight.

1995 was important to two local groups dedicated to entertaining the community. Seaford Amateur Dramatic Society celebrated fifty years' presenting all manner of plays, from its founding at the end of the Second World War as a social outlet for young men and women newly returned from war service. After appearing at a variety of venues in the town, in 1957 they made their headquarters at the Little Theatre in Steyne Road, where they continue to present a wide range of plays, winning several awards in drama festivals, with excellence both on- and back-stage.

Newly-formed in 1995 under the chairmanship of Stephen Newberry and with the support of South East Arts, who loaned two 16-mm projectors and made a £300 grant, Seaford Film Society also used the Little Theatre. The town had been without any cinema presentation

Programme cover, Cradle Hill C.P. School entertainment.

Seaford Dramatic Society, rehearsal of "Pools Paradise".

since the closure of the Ritz seventeen years before. A committee including David Tucknott (projectionist), Steve Benz, Nicholas and Angela Tredell, Krisztina Almasi, Jim Wethered and Denise Scott-Fears chose films to hire, dealt with publicity, fund-raising and all other aspects - not least the erecting and dismantling of the large screen. Their first screening on Saturday 27th May, was the Australian romantic comedy *"Strictly Ballroom"*. The Society's magazine "SeaScreen" has appeared at intervals since the first edition in July, 1995.

All that year, my search was on for a West Indian ex-service organisation comparable with the Canadians', so that they too could be represented in future "pilgrimages" to the cemetery, where nineteen of their compatriots were buried. This was achieved and each year since the ceremony has been attended by groups from both ex-service communities. The discovery of Irish soldiers' graves from the First World War has widened the scope of the remembrance ceremony even farther. In the same year, at the fifth attempt, the proposal that Seaford should have a Town Council was voted in: 4634 'yes' / 3755 'no' = majority of 879.

West Indian Ex-Servicemen's first attendance at Alfriston Road pilgrimage.

First "Clean Beach" award: junior Lifeguards bring flag ashore.

Throughout the period covered by this book, the local operatic society had continued presenting musical entertainments, gradually introducing more modern shows and fewer Gilbert and Sullivan, which had been the staple diet in earlier days. In the summer of 1996 they chose Cole Porter's *"Kiss me, Kate"*, loosely based on Shakespeare's *"The Taming of the Shrew"*. This amateur group gamely - and successfully - tackled a show with no less than seventeen featured numbers.

In 1997 Mr. Len Fisher became Seaford's first Town Manager, with an office at the Tourist Information Centre in Clinton Place. This appointment marked an upward move in the presentation of the town's image to the outside world, such success underlined when, on Seaford acquiring new status with a town council, it retained his services as Town Clerk. One of his first tasks was to promote the town's claim for a "Clean Beach" award, duly received in 1998. The success has been repeated each year since.

Seaford made television and national newspaper headlines when the Dutch training vessel *Eendracht*, attempting to leave Newhaven harbour under sail in a gale, was driven ashore at that black spot for shipwrecks, the beach opposite the ruins of Tide Mills village. Helicopters, lifeboats, police, coastguards, lifeguards - all converged to help the young crew ashore from the stricken ship, which was finally got off some time later.

In the last year of the century, two major events occurred that changed some aspects of the town forever. Accepted by referendum four years before, and with all legal, civic and practical arrangements in place, Seaford elected the members of its first-ever town council, with Cllr. Laurie Holland as Mayor. He was called on to represent the town on many occasions, and was one of the guests at the gala evening organised jointly by the Operatic and Film Societies to celebrate the re-opening of the Barn Theatre, complete with raked, upholstered seating for 138 patrons and new giant screen.

In a technological move to fight crime and monitor traffic, CCTV cameras were installed at relevant points in the town centre.

Thus I leave Seaford to its fate in the twenty-first century, and accounts of its later activities to some future historian.

Closed-circuit television (CCTV) mast near Seaford railway station.

Dr. Jill Rosser, Mayor of Seaford, unveils Millennium sun-dial.

BOOKS BY PATRICIA BERRY

Published by Seaford Museum:	THEN AND NOW IN SEAFORD
Published by European Library:	SEAFORD IN OLD PICTURE POSTCARDS
	ALFRISTON & DISTRICT IN OLD PICTURE POSTCARDS
	SEAFORD PAST AND PRESENT
Published by SB Publications:	SEAFORD & DISTRICT: A PORTRAIT IN OLD PICTURE POSTCARDS
	SEAFORD & DISTRICT: A PORTRAIT IN OLD PICTURE POSTCARDS VOL. 2
Published by Sutton Publishers:	SUTTON IN OLD PHOTOGRAPHS
	CHEAM & BELMONT IN OLD PHOTOGRAPHS
	THEATRICAL LONDON IN OLD PHOTOGRAPHS
	AROUND EPSOM IN OLD PHOTOGRAPHS
	EPSOM: THE TWENTIETH CENTURY
	A CENTURY OF SUTTON
	SURREY MEMORIES
(with Philip Pople)	BISHOPSTONE & SEAFORD IN OLD PHOTOGRAPHS
(with Philip Pople)	BISHOPSTONE & SEAFORD IN OLD PHOTOGRAPHS: A SECOND SELECTION
(with Kevin Gordon)	AROUND EASTBOURNE

ALSO numerous local history booklets for Seaford Museum. Since 1999 I have written a weekly column "From a Seaford Album" for the local edition of the Sussex Express & County Herald.

ABOUT PATRICIA BERRY

Born and raised in Inner Surrey, Pat's early claim to fame was that, during the flying-bomb raids of the Second World War, she was several times the only pupil out of five hundred to be in school.

After a career in various branches of the law, she came to Seaford in 1959 as wife of the local blacksmith. Widowed in her mid-fifties, she turned her interest in local history (reinforced by active membership of Seaford Museum) to writing and lecturing on the subject, and has in recent years become an enthusiastic tutor of adult students for the Workers' Educational Association.

As "Dee Berry", she was for eighteen years the local agent for the Theatregoers Club of Great Britain (till its closure in 2002) and reckons to have conducted members to more than three hundred West End and provincial shows and travelled some 40,000 miles around Europe with them.